P9-DBP-343

EIGHT WHO WRESTLED DEATH

EIGHT WHO WRESTLED DEATH

Ned Gold

Illustrated by Tom Antonishak

940.54
GoL
8894

Blairsville Junior High School
Blairsville, Pennsylvania

RAINTREE PUBLISHERS
Milwaukee • Toronto • Melbourne • London

Copyright © 1980, Raintree Publishers Inc.

All rights reserved. No part of this book may be reproduced
or utilized in any form or by any means, electronic or mechanical,
including photocopying, recording, or by an information storage
and retrieval system, without permission in writing from the
Publisher. Inquiries should be addressed to Raintree Publishers Inc.,
205 West Highland Avenue, Milwaukee, Wisconsin 53203.

Library of Congress Number: 79-23215

2 3 4 5 6 7 8 9 0 84 83 82 81

Printed and bound in the United States of America.

Library of Congress Cataloging in Publication Data

Gold, Ned.
  Eight who wrestled death.

  SUMMARY: Eddie Rickenbacker and his crew struggle to
survive when their plane crashes in the Pacific Ocean
while on their way to deliver a top secret message to
General MacArthur.
  1. World War, 1939-1945 — Aerial operations, American
— Juvenile Literature.   2. Rickenbacker, Edward Vernon,
1890-1973 — Juvenile literature. [1. World War, 1939-
1945 — Aerial operations, American.   2. Rickenbacker,
Edward Vernon, 1890-1973.   3. Survival]
  I. Antonishak, Tom. II. Title.
D790.G64   940.54′49′73   79-23215

ISBN 0-8172-1554-9 lib. bdg.

CONTENTS

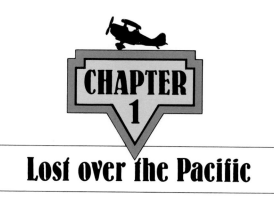

CHAPTER 1

Lost over the Pacific

It was 1942. The United States had just entered World War II. The secretary of war, Henry Stimson, wanted to inspect the Air Force bases in the United States. The armed forces in those bases were being trained to fight in the war. And Stimson had to know just how good the officers and ground crews were. He also wanted a report on their fighting spirit. It was a top secret mission, and the person who went on the mission had to know a lot about aviation. That person was Eddie Rickenbacker.

Rickenbacker was especially good for the task. He had long experience with flying. He was the president of Eastern Air Lines and had been an ace combat pilot in World War I. To many Americans the name Rickenbacker meant aviation.

He was born in Columbus, Ohio, in 1890.

When his father died, the family was left with almost no money. Eddie had to go to work to help support his mother and the other seven children in the family.

Although he was only eleven years old at the time, Eddie held a full-time job at a factory. As time went by, he got better jobs at more pay. Eddie finally ended up working in an automobile manufacturing company. It was there that he developed an interest in cars and began to study automotive engineering.

He had just turned to professional auto racing when World War I broke out. Eddie went into the armed forces and was sent to France. There, he became the chauffeur to General Pershing.

But Eddie's dream was to fly. His dream came true when he was approved for admission into the air service. By the time the war was over, Rickenbacker had shot down twenty-two German planes and had become the leading American combat pilot. For his brave exploits, he was awarded the Congressional Medal of Honor.

Returning home from the war, he raised enough money through various business ventures to purchase Eastern Air Lines, and become its president and general manager.

So, Eddie was an ideal person to send on the secret mission. In one month, Eddie visited

forty-three bases. The mission was successful, and Stimson decided to send Rickenbacker on another top secret mission. This time he was to go to bases all over the world.

His first stops were England, Ireland, and Iceland. Next, Rickenbacker, along with his old friend Colonel Hans Adamson, was to go to the South Pacific. Their trip would include visits to Australia, New Guinea, and Guadalcanal. But their first stop was Hawaii, where they were to get their airplane and crew for the mission.

Eddie and Hans arrived in Honolulu, Hawaii, and found that they would be flying in an old four-engine Boeing Flying Fortress. The plane was due to be returned to the States to be used for training. Eddie had hoped that they would be using one of the new B-24 bombers, but because they were all being used in action, the Fortress was the only long-range plane available to them.

The crew they would be traveling with were all experienced members of the Army Transport Command. The pilot was Captain Cherry, a colorful character who dressed in cowboy boots and wore a goatee. His copilot was Lieutenant Whittaker who, next to Rickenbacker and Adamson (who were both in their fifties), was the oldest man on the crew. The navigator, flight engineer, and radioman were all in their twenties.

In addition, they would be carrying an extra

passenger. He was a ground crew chief named Sergeant Alex, who was returning to his unit in Australia.

Several stacks of high-priority mail for the various headquarters that would be inspected were also aboard.

Part of Eddie's mission was to deliver a top secret message. He had been given the message from Secretary of War Stimson to be delivered to General Douglas MacArthur. The message was so secret that it could not be written down, for fear that it might fall into enemy hands. Stimson gave the message to Rickenbacker verbally. Eddie memorized it and was expected to pass it on to General MacArthur in the same way.

As the eight men took off in the Fortress, everything seemed to be going right. It was a beautiful, star-studded night, and the moon shone brilliantly over the blue Pacific.

"I hope the weather will be like this all the way," Eddie told Captain Cherry.

"Don't worry," he was reassured by Cherry. "It will be."

They flew through the night without incident. But as daylight broke and Eddie began looking for Canton Island, where they were to refuel before continuing on across the Pacific, he began to worry. He did not see the island coming into view.

Could they have overshot the island during the night? The thought occurred to him that they may have been flying faster than they had realized. It was much later that they found out what had happened. The tailwind was really three times stronger than they had been told, and it had pushed them beyond the island.

Eddie voiced his fears to Captain Cherry. "How much gas do we have?" he asked.

Cherry checked the gauge and reported, "A little over four hours' worth."

Rickenbacker hoped that this would be enough to last until they found the island. But he could not help feeling that they were headed for trouble.

When the island had not come into view after about two hours, Captain Cherry nosed the plane down to fly lower. The radio engineer called Canton Island to get a bearing. But they answered that they did not have the equipment to do this.

It was now clear to everyone aboard that they had passed Canton Island and were lost somewhere over the Pacific. In one last attempt to find the island Cherry turned the plane in almost every direction, but with no luck. Several times, someone thought they had seen it, but it was only a mirage. They had been looking for land so hard that they seemed to see it where there was none. This is what is called "island eyes."

"How much gas now?" Rickenbacker asked.

"About an hour's worth," Cherry replied.

Time was running out, and now the possibility of a crash landing seemed sure.

CHAPTER 2

Here It Comes

The radio operator continued to call for bearings but still had no luck. Captain Cherry turned off the two outboard engines in order to save fuel.

"Send an SOS," he ordered. But even though the radioman beat out the message several times, there was no answer.

To make the plane lighter for the crash, everything movable had to be thrown overboard immediately. This included the high-priority mail sacks, the baggage, and personal belongings of all sorts.

The crew put on their Mae West life jackets and filled thermos bottles with water and coffee. They also got the emergency food rations. Next they propped mattresses against the bulkheads to soften the shock of the landing. Then came the wait for the crash. It was only a short wait, but to the eight men aboard the plane it seemed like hours.

Captain Cherry dipped the plane into a long

glide, and as the men looked out the windows, they could see the ocean coming closer and closer.

The tension was unbearable. "How much longer?" someone cried.

"Hold on!" shouted Rickenbacker. "Here it comes!"

With a thunderous roar, the men were jolted forward. Water began gushing through the broken windows. Cherry had made a perfect crash landing. If he had not timed it as perfecty as he had, the plane would have hit the crest of a wave instead of its slope, and all could have been killed.

But there was no time to think of anything now except getting out as quickly as possible.

Rickenbacker made his way out onto one of the wings and began helping the others out. Three bright yellow life rafts had automatically inflated. There were two large rafts and one smaller one.

15

The rough waters made it difficult to get into the rafts.

After everyone had his place in the rafts, the strong wind pushed them away from the plane.

"Hey, where's the water?" someone called.

They realized that with the terror and confusion of the crash, they had left behind the thermos bottles of water, as well as the emergency rations.

"Let's go back and get them."

"No!" Rickenbacker ordered. "It's too dangerous! The plane is sinking much too fast."

But this turned out to be a mistake. The plane stayed afloat for another six minutes, which would have given them enough time to return and get the items they needed.

The wind carried them farther and farther from the plane. The eight men in three life boats watched as the tail of the ship sprung upright and then disappeared beneath the waters of the Pacific.

There were three men in each of the two larger rafts and two men in the smaller one. They took stock of their provisions. Although some of the men had chocolate bars, they had become soaked and could not be eaten. All that they had to keep them alive were four oranges.

Everyone was badly shaken up by the crash, and several of the men became seasick with the violent bobbing of the life boats. As they looked down into the dark water around them, they could see the long, menacing shapes of sharks swimming around them.

As the sun went down and darkness came, Eddie assigned the men to two-hour watches.

"I'll offer the first man to spot land, a ship, or a plane a hundred dollars," he called. The rocking motion made them feel as if they were constantly being doused with buckets of water and they were kept awake by the movement of the sharks banging against the bottom of the life boats. On that first night, no one slept. They were too wet and miserable. And they were frightened at what lay ahead of them.

The next morning, Rickenbacker carefully divided the first orange into eight equal parts and passed them around. It was possible that this tiny meal would have to last them several days, and they ate every bit of the food, including the seeds and the rind.

Although they were upset at not having any water, Eddie warned them: "Whatever you do, don't drink any ocean water. The salt will drive you crazy with thirst."

A calm fell over the sea, and the sun beat down fiercely. There was no escape from it, no shade anywhere. Since the men had left most of their clothing aboard the plane, in order to make their escape easier, shelter from the burning rays was almost impossible.

Their skin turned raw and red. Their hands became swollen and blistered. When the salt-water got into the wounds that some of them suffered during the crash, the flesh began to burn and crack. Their mouths became covered with sores.

Eddie, however, had brought along his hat, which he would fill with water and then pull down over his ears. This kept him cool.

The nights were cold and dense, with a thick mist surrounding the rafts. Eddie tried to get as much rest as possible, but he was kept awake by cries and moans from the other men. Now and then he heard the sound of a prayer.

The smallness of the rafts made it impossible for any of them to stretch out completely. Every time one man moved, the others in the boat had to change positions.

Three days passed. No one had any idea where they were. They continued to drift aimlessly on the wide Pacific.

CHAPTER 3

A Bit of Luck

On the fourth morning, the second orange was divided. The men shared what was only their second meal in seventy-two hours. What made their small meal seem even smaller were the hundreds of fish they could see swimming about the rafts. If only they could catch them . . .

Eddie did try to catch one. He saved a piece of orange peel from his meal and used it as bait. But the fish would have no part of it.

Time began to pass even more slowly. At times, the rafts actually seemed to be standing still. Only by watching the sun at dawn and noting that each day it rose later and later did the men know that they were still moving.

Every night, Captain Cherry sent up a flare. Eddie and the others watched for some sign that it had been seen by someone long after its light had disappeared. But they watched in vain.

Although Eddie had warned the men about

drinking the salty seawater, he awoke one night to find that the passenger, Sergeant Alex, was thirstily gulping water from the sea. Although Eddie at first stormed at him, he realized that the man was very ill. Sergeant Alex began to sink into a delirium. He was talking on and on without making any sense.

The other crew member who was sharing the

two-man raft with Sergeant Alex tried to make him more comfortable by shielding him from the sun. But there was no shade anywhere and Sergeant Alex's condition grew steadily worse.

Some of the other men began to get sick as well. Eddie decided that the time had come to eat the remaining oranges. On the sixth day, they shared the last of their meager food, and they prayed that someone would spot them soon.

The men began to talk of nothing but food. They described their favorite meals and planned the first thing they would eat after they had been rescued.

"Don't talk about it so much!" cautioned Rickenbacker. "Try not to even think about food. It will only make you feel hungrier."

After several more days, almost all talk stopped. The men were simply too weak. They would lie baking in the unbearable heat of the sun, too sick to speak or move.

Every morning and evening, the men moved the rafts together to form a triangle. Prayers were said, and hymns were sung. One of the men had saved a Bible from the plane, and psalms were also read.

On the eighth day, a small miracle occurred. And even the men who were not religious felt that maybe the prayers had done some good.

During the afternoon of that day, the men were

lying motionless in the rafts, as usual. There was a great stillness on the water. Nothing was moving.

Eddie was sitting in his raft with his old hat pulled down over his ears to keep himself as cool as possible. Suddenly, he felt something land on top of his head. Instinct told him that it was a seagull.

He knew that this was their one chance for survival. If he missed this chance to catch some food, who knew when they would have another chance.

Carefully, inch by inch, he raised his arm. Then suddenly, with a quick motion, he grabbed for the bird's neck, caught it, and twisted.

Food at last!

The seagull's feathers were removed, and it was carved into equal parts, which were quickly and hungrily eaten by the men. They didn't mind the salty taste of the raw bird.

The seagull turned out to be a lucky omen. They used a few small bits that were left as bait. They were able to catch two fish with the seagull bait.

Despite their lack of water, everyone felt better immediately, even Sergeant Alex. And their spirits were lifted.

That night, as they were sleeping, the men were jolted awake by a violently quaking beneath the rafts. The wind whipped around them fiercely. This could mean only one thing. Rain was on its way! The seagull had brought them more good luck.

As the first long-awaited drops began to fall, the men opened their mouths and drank thirstily. They were instantly refreshed. Then they gathered some handkerchiefs and other pieces of cloth. They used the cloth to soak up rainwater, which they put into buckets. Once this storm was over, there was no telling when there would be another one.

Even when one of the rafts turned over during the squall, their spirits remained high. With strength they didn't know they had after nine long days drifting on the ocean, they set it right.

The storm was over as suddenly as it had begun. It had lasted for only twenty minutes, but it brought them enough water to last for another several days, if they used it wisely.

Even with food and water in his system, however, Sergeant Alex continued to get worse. He was moved into Eddie's raft so that Eddie could look after him more closely. Rickenbacker held him tightly to his body, trying to give some warmth to the frail body that trembled with chills.

But on the morning of the thirteenth day, it was all over for Sergeant Alex. He had put up a brave fight, but he had lost his battle for survival.

A short burial service was said, and his body was rolled over the side of the raft.

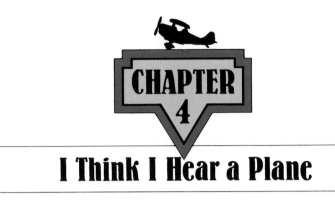

CHAPTER 4

I Think I Hear a Plane

Sharks were all around the three little boats. They would come up under them and hit them suddenly and sharply. The men were saved by the fact that the sharks' mouths were round, and they could not get their teeth into the rafts.

The water from the storm was now gone, and the sun continued to beat down mercilessly. The men did manage to hook a shark. But after it had been carved and its sections passed around, the men found that they could not swallow raw shark meat even though they were starving.

Unfortunately, while he was carving up the shark, Captain Cherry punctured a hole in the bottom of his raft. Water began to spurt through, and he was not able to patch it properly. He and the men who shared his raft constantly had to bail out the water that seeped through.

Rickenbacker's friend Adamson began to complain of pains in his back, and Eddie grew depressed at the thought that his old friend might be the next to go. To see him suffering, in pain, his skin burned red by the sun, was an unbearable sight for Eddie.

Rickenbacker knew that the morale of the men was at an all-time low. He tried to encourage them with his philosophy, which he learned on the battlefields of France during World War I. "The harder we fight now," he told his men, "and the more we have to go through, the sweeter the relief will be after it's all over." He was disappointed when the dejected men did not see his point of view.

So, he decided to use another trick on them.

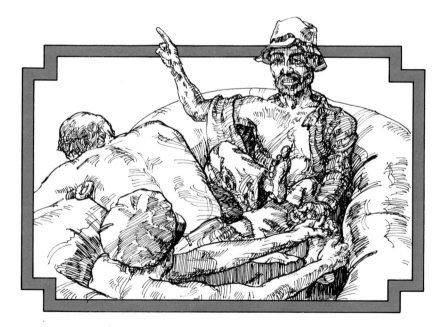

He would shock them out of depression. He did this by snarling at them, picking on every little thing that they did, hurling insults right and left.

Later, he overheard one of the men saying to another, "I'd like to live long enough just to see that mean so-and-so Eddie Rickenbacker buried at sea." He knew the trick had worked!

Eddie was himself in great pain. Shortly before he began this mission, he had been in a plane crash in Atlanta. He had nearly died, and he was not completely healed.

The men grew thinner and thinner. And as their strength weakened, they thought that they saw ships on the horizon and planes in the sky. The motion of the sea and the bright white light of the sun had confused their senses. At times, the sight of seagulls made them think that they were close to land. But Rickenbacker told them that these birds sometimes appeared far out on the ocean, where no land was near.

The point of their compass had rusted, along with the watches that some of them wore. Still, they could tell what time it was by watching the sun. The winds sometimes turned the rafts around and drove them in an opposite direction, but they noted that they were headed southwest most of the time.

Eddie thought that they might have a better chance of being spotted if they headed southeast.

He was determined not to give up the fight to deliver his secret message to General MacArthur.

Something had to be done. Rickenbacker hit upon the idea of sending one of the rafts off on its own. The three strongest men would try to beat the current and set off to the southeast. Cherry volunteered. And with two others, he got into one of the boats.

They began paddling away from the two other rafts. But, although there was only a light wind and each of the men took turns paddling, a day later they were still in sight of the others. Cherry had to return. And Eddie had to abandon the plan. This was a great disappointment for all the men. They had been looking forward to the plan as their last chance of being spotted. Now, it seemed as if all hope was lost.

But this failure marked a turning point in the fortunes of the survivors. From then on, a squall occurred practicaly every day. They were able to get enough water to live on. The problem of thirst had been solved.

As the fourth week of their ordeal began, a remarkable thing happened.

One night, as he was dozing off in his raft, Rickenbacker thought that he noticed streaks of light gleaming against the pitch black water. At first he thought that his eyes were playing tricks on him again. But then he realized that what he had seen was a school of fish.

A pack of sharks had attacked the school, and the rafts were directly in the middle of their battleground. The mysterious streaks of light were mackerel shooting out of the water trying to get away from the sharks.

To Rickenbacker's amazement, one of the fish jumped all the way out of the water and landed at his feet in the raft. He jumped on it before it could flop out of the boat again. Another fish landed in Cherry's raft. The men had not eaten anything for nearly a week, and they were overjoyed at their good fortune. The fish gave them enough food to last for two days.

The squalls continued with greater force, and the rafts spun around in practically every direction. It was impossible to get any rest, since the boats were tilting and wobbling with every motion of the stormy sea.

One afternoon, weak from exhaustion, Eddie

heard Cherry calling to him. "I think I hear a plane!" At first, Eddie thought that it was another trick of his imagination. But the sound grew louder and louder.

The men all turned to look in the direction it seemed to be coming from and, about five miles away, they all saw the same thing. A plane!

Help was on the way, at last.

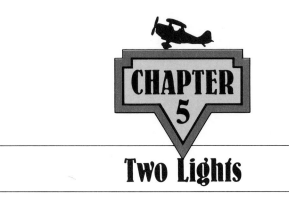

CHAPTER 5

Two Lights

All seven survivors stood up in the rafts and began shouting their lungs out. They waved their arms wildly in an attempt to get the pilot's attention.

But a squall came between them and the plane, and they lost sight of it.

"Don't be disappointed," Eddie tried to cheer them. "If we saw one, we'll see another. This only means that we've drifted within reach of help. Have a little patience."

He was right. The next day, they spotted two more planes. Again, they hollered and waved their shirts in the air furiously. But they knew that all this energy was useless. The planes were too far away. To the pilots, they would be practically invisible against the ocean.

The next morning, four more planes appeared, but that afternoon there were none. They waited expectantly for the sound of engines, but none came. They feared that they had drifted past land and were headed for the open sea again.

They were somewhat cheered by the fact that food was now within reach. They had mastered the trick of scooping up some of the hundreds of sardine-like fish that gathered around the rafts each morning just before dawn.

With some of their strength returned, the men began to grow restless. Where were the planes that had given them their brief moment of hope? When would they return?

Captain Cherry was especially anxious to take matters into his own hands.

"I want to take the smallest raft myself," he told Rickenbacker. "It's useless to just sit here and wait until we're spotted. It might never happen."

"What do you want to do that for?" Rickenbacker asked him.

"So the rafts will be scattered. It might give us a better chance of being seen," Cherry told him.

Rickenbacker tried to reason with him. "But if the planes couldn't see three rafts bunched together, how do you think they're going to spot just one tiny one?"

Cherry was determined to go it alone. "But I won't do it unless it's OK with you," he told Eddie.

Rickenbacker knew that to prolong the argument any longer might lead to trouble. Tensions

were already beginning to grow. Although he still thought that it was a mistake, Eddie told Cherry, "OK. Go ahead. And good luck."

Cherry took the smallest raft and drifted off alone. As the six other survivors watched, a breeze carried the little life boat with the small figure in it out of sight.

This spurred three of the other men to demand that they too be allowed to try such a plan. Eddie now saw that it was useless to try to keep the rafts together.

Perhaps the men were right. Maybe they did have a better chance of being spotted if they were spread out. He let the other three men go, leaving his raft alone. In it were the two weakest survivors, his friend Adamson, and the flight engineer, Bartek, who was too ill even to raise his head to drink.

Bartek could only summon up enough strength now and again to whisper, "Have the planes come back yet?"

The next afternoon, two planes did come back. And although Rickenbacker was the only one in his life boat with enough strength to stand up and try to get their attention, he did it with the energy of three men. Night was beginning to fall, and he knew that this was their last chance of being spotted that day.

Furiously he waved and shouted, but the planes passed by. Depressed, he sat down again in the

raft and got ready to face another long night lost at sea.

Only several minutes had passed, however, when he heard the sound of engines again. The two planes were returning. Could this mean that they had spotted him after all?

This time, even Adamson and Bartek started shouting. And one of the planes made a low circle around the raft. Eddie noticed with joy that it was a U.S. Navy single-engine pontoon plane.

After circling once the plane took off after its mate.

"What's happening?" Bartek wanted to know. "Where are they going?"

"Are they coming back?" asked Adamson.

Rickenbacker assured them. "They'll be back. They know where we are now."

The minutes passed. It seemed like an eternity to Rickenbacker, Adamson, and Bartek. They worried that night might fall before the planes had a chance to get back to them. They knew that they would have little chance of being spotted in the dark.

Almost an hour went by before the planes appeared again. The sun was setting. Both planes flew above the rafts, and then one left while the other circled the life boat.

But why wouldn't it land? Eddie continued to yell and jump about the boat, thinking perhaps that the Navy pilot thought that the raft was carrying three dead men.

As night fell, the plane was still circling overhead.

Then, a flash of bright white light. A flare from the plane. This was followed by a bright red light. It was obviously a signal.

"He's waiting for a boat!" Eddie yelled to his two comrades with relief. "He's sending them a code."

Far out on the horizon, two lights blinked a return signal. The end of their long ordeal was near.

CHAPTER 6

Safe at Last

Carefully, the plane landed on the surface of the ocean a few yards from the raft. Rickenbacker paddled the life boat up to the plane and caught hold of the pontoon.

The pilot and the radio operator climbed down to help them. Eddie was never so glad to see anybody in his entire life.

"I can't show another light," the pilot told Rickenbacker. "There might be some Japanese nearby. A PT boat is on its way out, but instead of waiting here, let's taxi back to it."

Since the plane had only enough room for one passenger, Rickenbacker insisted that Adamson, the weakest of the three survivors, have the seat.

"But you're coming along too," the pilot told him. "It's too dangerous, the enemy is all around us."

"But where are you going to put us?"

"On the wing, of course," the pilot said with a smile.

The pilot and the radioman hoisted Bartek onto the right wing and tied him to it, with his legs dangling over the side. Rickenbacker was securely attached to the left wing, and the plane taxied for about half an hour to the waiting PT boat.

Rickenbacker and Bartek were put aboard, but it was decided that another move might be fatal for Adamson, so he stayed in the plane, which continued on to the base.

Aboard the boat, Eddie heard good news about the other survivors.

Captain Cherry had been spotted that afternoon by a plane and had been picked up by another PT boat. The three men in the second raft had washed up on the beach of an uninhabited island several miles away. And help had

been sent to them as soon as they had been spotted.

Satisfied that his comrades were alive and well, Eddie turned his attention to himself. All he could think of was water. He drank thirstily almost the whole way back to the base.

At the base, he and Bartek were taken to a small one-room hospital. Rickenbacker discovered that he had lost almost forty pounds during the ordeal. When he saw his reflection in a mirror, he was horrified.

He was shown the headlines of newspapers that had reported news of his death. It was a strange feeling for him to read his own obituary.

He was anxious to get back to his wife and children. But first he had his mission to complete. When he was well enough to travel, he flew to Australia and was met by General MacArthur personally when the plane landed.

It was then that he got to deliver his secret message. It had been delayed, but Eddie had never given up the fight to complete his assignment.

The incredible ordeal on a raft in the middle of the wide Pacific had not been in vain. Although one man had died, everyone else had come through.

On that dusty airfield in Australia, a remarkable story of courage and survival had finally come to a close.